Rocks, Gems, and Minerals

Rocks, Gems, and Minerals

Lisa Sita

Thomson Learning

New York

A FRIEDMAN GROUP BOOK

First published in the
United States in 1995 by
Thomson Learning
New York, NY

Library of Congress Cataloging-in-Publication Data
   Sita, Lisa, date
         Rocks. gems, and minerals / Lisa Sita.
            p.   cm.— (Exploring science)
         Includes bibliographical references and index.
         ISBN 1-56847-269-2
            1. Geology—Juvenile literature.   [1. Geology.]
   I. Title.   II. Series: Exploring science (New York, N.Y.)
   QE29.S54   1995
   552—dc20
                                                      94-43975
                                                        CIP
                                                         AC

EXPLORING SCIENCE: ROCKS, GEMS, AND MINERALS
was prepared and produced by
Michael Friedman Publishing Group, Inc.
15 West 26th Street
New York, New York 10010

Editor: Nathaniel Marunas
Art Director/Designer: Jeff Batzli
Layout: Jonathan Gaines
Photography Director: Christopher Bain
Photography Researchers: Christopher Bain and Susan Mettler
Illustrations: George Gilliland

Front Cover Illustration: George Gilliland
Back Cover Photography: (clockwise from top left):
©Edward Degginger/Bruce Coleman, ©Brian Skyum/FPG International,
Smithsonian Institution, Science VU/Visuals Unlimited

Color separations by Benday Scancolour Co. Ltd.
Printed in China.

Dedication
For Grandma Angie

Acknowledgments
The author offers her sincere thanks to her friends and colleagues in the Education Department of the American Museum of Natural History, especially Karen Lund, Brad Burnham, Jay Holmes, Stephanie Fins, and Marcia White; Nathaniel Marunas and Jeff Batzli of Michael Friedman Publishing; Kelly Matthews; Thomson Learning; and friends and family members, especially Joey, Stephanie, Tonie-Ann, and Manny, for their patience and support during the writing of this book.

TABLE OF CONTENTS

INTRODUCTION

A LIVING, CHANGING PLANET

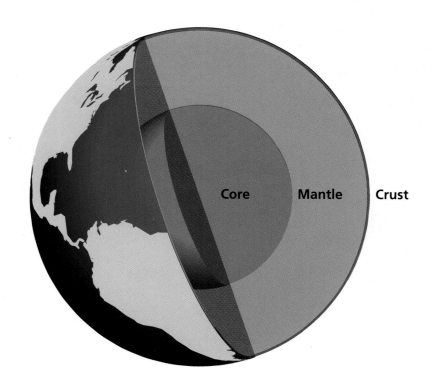

Core   Mantle   Crust

EARTH WAS FORMED ABOUT 4.5 BILLION YEARS AGO; ITS THREE BASIC LAYERS ARE THE CORE, MANTLE, AND CRUST. THIS DIAGRAM SHOWS THE RELATIVE THICKNESSES OF EACH LAYER.

Earth from the Inside Out

core (diameter) = 4,300 miles (6,919 kilometers)

mantle (from core to crust) = 1,786 miles (2,874 kilometers)

crust (from mantle to surface) = 19 miles (31 kilometers)

OPPOSITE: A VIEW OF PLANET EARTH FROM OUTER SPACE.

THE BIRTH OF OUR PLANET

Earth is an active, ever-changing planet full of colorful landscapes teeming with life. Earth was formed about 4.5 billion years ago when stray particles floating in the universe clumped together into a massive ball of matter. The heaviest particles, those of **iron** and **nickel**, sank to the center of the planet and formed a **core**. The Earth's **mantle**, a thick layer of hot molten rock, formed around the core, and a **crust** (the Earth's thinnest layer) formed over the liquid rock. Since it was first formed, Earth has gone through many physical changes. And although our home planet looks very different now than it did in its early life, Earth still has a core, a mantle, and a crust.

The entire Earth is about 7,910 miles (12,727 kilometers) in diameter. Its core, from end to end, measures about 4,300 miles (6,919 kilometers). Its mantle, from the outer surface of the core to the inner surface of the crust, averages about 1,786 miles (2,874 kilometers). Yet the crust, the layer of the Earth that is the most active, is only about 19 miles (31 kilometers) thick.

Earth's Changing Crust

You can experiment with how plate tectonics causes the Earth's crust to change.

You will need: several differently colored slabs of modeling clay.

1. Press each color of clay into a flat sheet.

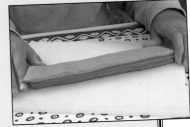

2. Lay the sheets one on top of another.

3. Hold the layered clay at both ends and push toward the middle. The clay will start to bend in the middle.

4. Continue to push. The clay will fold. Eventually, if you continue to push, the fold will tear.

In this experiment, each sheet of clay represents a layer of rock in the earth's crust. Your hands play the role of the pressure caused by the Earth's shifting plates. When the Earth's crust bends as the layered clay did in step 3, the bends that form valleys are called **synclines**, and the bends that form peaks are called **anticlines**. When the crust folds as it did in step 4, it is called an **overfold**. When the overfold tears, it is called a **faulted fold**.

EARTH'S ACTIVE CRUST

Earth's crust has been continually changing since the Earth was first formed. Mountains have risen up. Continents have broken apart and drifted from one another. **Glaciers** (enormous bodies of ice) have slowly traveled across these continents over the ages, carving out valleys and creating new landscapes by picking up, pushing, and depositing rocks and dirt. In fact, the Earth's crust is still changing. And while some of the changes happen so slowly that we don't even notice them, other changes—such as earthquakes and volcanic eruptions—are quick and dramatic.

Changes in the Earth's crust happen because of two things—**erosion** and **plate tectonics**. Erosion is the slow wearing away of the land by natural forces such as rain, wind, and the movement of bodies of water. In much the same way that an artist sculpts a statue, wind and water sculpt landscapes out of the living rock.

ABOVE, RIGHT: THESE MAJESTIC PEAKS IN CHAMONIX, IN THE FRENCH ALPS, AROSE DUE TO THE SHIFTING OF THE EARTH'S PLATES. ABOVE: MOVING WATER IS ONE AGENT OF EROSION. HERE, OCEAN WAVES BREAK FORCEFULLY AGAINST A CLIFF IN OREGON.

For example, waves hitting a cliff by the sea will eventually wear away part of the cliff, just like playing in the schoolyard will eventually wear away the soles of a person's sneakers. But, unlike sneakers, it will take thousands of years before the cliff starts to look different. Erosion wears down part of the landscape and carries away the residue to other parts of the Earth's crust. This means that as one part of the Earth is wearing away, another part is building up. This is one way in which the Earth's crust is constantly changing.

The Earth's crust is not a continuous covering of rock. It is cracked in many places, forming huge pieces called **plates** that float on top of Earth's liquid mantle. The cracks are called **faults**. The movement of the plates is called **plate tectonics**.

The earth's plates move slowly and, over millions of years, have changed the way the Earth looks by shifting continents around.

Floating Plates

The **theory of plate tectonics** explains that the Earth's crust is cracked in many places, forming huge pieces, or plates, that float on the molten rock of the Earth's mantle. This movement of the plates causes mountains to form, continents to shift, earthquakes to occur, and volcanoes to erupt.

A Hot Discovery

Companies drilling into the Earth's crust for oil have found that the temperature goes up as they drill from the surface down. Every 20 feet into the crust, the temperature rises 1 degree Fahrenheit (or 1 degree Celsius for every 35 meters).

A VOLCANO ERUPTS ON THE ISLAND OF HAWAII, CAUSING A GUSHING FLOW OF LAVA.

Sometimes the plates bump into one another with such force that the edges of the plates are pushed upward, causing mountains to form. Sometimes when the plates hit each other they lock together. This causes pressure to build up. When the pressure is finally released and the plates unlock, earthquakes occur. Other times when the plates collide, one plate will push the edge of another plate down into the mantle. This allows some of the hot liquid rock from the mantle, called **magma**, to escape into the crust, causing volcanoes to form and erupt. Volcanoes and earthquakes both happen in areas where there are faults.

The Grand Canyon: A Lesson in Earth History

One of the most spectacular examples of what erosion does to the Earth's crust is the Grand Canyon in Arizona. The wearing away of this landscape has exposed many layers of rocks, the oldest of which date from more than 2 billion years ago. Each period of time in the Earth's history has a name. The oldest rocks exposed in the Grand Canyon date back to a period in geologic history called the Precambrian.

The **Precambrian Era**—over 570 million years ago (m.y.a.)

The **Paleozoic Era**—570 m.y.a. to 245 m.y.a.:
The Cambrian Period—570 to 510 m.y.a.
The Ordovician Period—510 to 439 m.y.a.
The Silurian Period—439 to 408 m.y.a.
The Devonian Period—408 to 362 m.y.a.
The Mississippian Period—362 to 323 m.y.a.
The Pennsylvanian Period—323 to 290 m.y.a.
The Permian Period—290 to 245 m.y.a.

The Mesozoic Era—245 m.y.a. to 65 m.y.a.:
The Triassic Period—245 to 208 m.y.a.
The Jurassic Period—208 to 146 m.y.a.
The Cretaceous Period—146 to 65 m.y.a.

The Cenozoic Era—65 m.y.a. to the present:
The Tertiary Period—65 to 1.8 m.y.a.
The Quaternary Period—1.8 m.y.a. to the present

EARTH'S HISTORY IS DIVIDED INTO TIME PERIODS, AS SHOWN HERE. WE CAN TELL WHEN LAYERS OF ROCKS WERE FORMED BY EXAMINING WHERE THEY LIE IN THE EARTH'S CRUST.

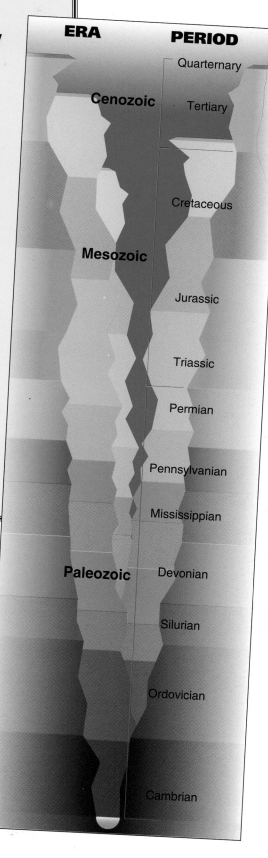

ERA	PERIOD
Cenozoic	Quarternary
	Tertiary
Mesozoic	Cretaceous
	Jurassic
	Triassic
Paleozoic	Permian
	Pennsylvanian
	Mississippian
	Devonian
	Silurian
	Ordovician
	Cambrian

THE GRAND CANYON IN ARIZONA, WHERE EROSION (CAUSED PRIMARILY BY THE COLORADO RIVER, WHICH FLOWS FROM THE SNOWFIELDS OF WYOMING TO THE GULF OF CALIFORNIA IN MEXICO) HAS EXPOSED MANY LAYERS OF ROCK. MUCH OF THE CANYON IS PROTECTED BY THE FEDERAL GOVERMENT, MAKING IT AN EXCELLENT SITE TO STUDY EARTH'S GEOLOGIC HISTORY.

HUMAN BEINGS HAVE BEEN USING THE EARTH'S MINERALS FOR THOUSANDS OF YEARS. HERE, MODERN-DAY MACHINERY IS USED TO CARRY RUBBLE AWAY FROM A COPPER MINE IN NEW MEXICO.

Lyell's Contribution

Charles Lyell was one of the first people to express the idea that the Earth's crust is, and always has been, slowly and continually changing. Lyell published his thoughts in the three-volume work *Principles of Geology* between 1830 and 1833.

A WORLD OF COLOR

As we walk along the surface of the crust, we find a rainbow of differently colored and variously shaped rocks all around us. When we walk along a beach, past a stream, through a canyon, or along a mountain trail, what do we often find beneath our feet? We feel sand sifting through our toes. We see pebbles polished smooth by running water. We hear soil crunching beneath our boots. All of these things, as well as the canyon walls and moun-

tain peaks that beautify our hike, are made up of the basic materials that form the Earth's crust—rocks and minerals.

Even in cities we are surrounded by the rich resources that are taken from the uppermost layer of our planet. The trains, cars, and buses that we travel in are made of metals mined from the Earth. Our schools, apartment buildings, banks, and libraries are built from **granite**, **limestone**, and other rocks quarried from the ground. Rocks are used to make the concrete that our streets

and sidewalks are made of. And some chalkboards in our classrooms are made of a rock called **slate**.

The Earth's crust is made of various kinds of rock, from its surface right down to where the plates float on the mantle. Rocks are made of minerals. What are these hard materials on which we depend for so much?

CHAPTER ONE

MINERALS

SOMETIMES, CRYSTALS OF DIFFERENT MINERALS ARE CLOSE TOGETHER WHEN THEY FORM, SO THEY APPEAR TO BE PART OF THE SAME SUBSTANCE, LIKE THESE CRYSTALS OF PYRITE AND QUARTZ.

Minerals in Food

Our bodies and the foods we eat contain tiny amounts of minerals, called trace minerals. Some foods are rich in certain trace minerals. Nuts, for example, are rich in copper, manganese, and zinc. Oats and coconuts are rich in sulfur, and spinach and sunflower seeds are rich in iron.

MINERALS ALL AROUND US

Minerals are everywhere. They are even present in our bodies in very tiny amounts, called **trace minerals**. They are found in the foods we eat and the water we drink. When someone at the dinner table asks you to pass the salt, they are actually asking you to pass the mineral **halite**. When you brush your teeth, the mineral **fluorite** in your toothpaste helps you to fight cavities. And when you sprinkle powder on your body after a bath, you are dusting yourself with the mineral **talc**. A mineral is a nonliving,

natural substance found in the Earth that has certain physical and chemical characteristics. Minerals are usually found in **crystal** form. This means that the basic

HALITE.

shape of a particular mineral will always be the same, regardless of where in the world the mineral is found. **Pyrite**, for example, has a cubic crystal shape—it occurs in nature as a six-sided cube. If you break a piece of pyrite into smaller pieces, each one of those smaller pieces would also be a six-sided cube.

FLUORITE.

Make Your Own Crystals

This project will give you an opportunity to observe a crystal as it "grows." Because you need to use the oven, make sure that an adult helps you complete this project.

You will need: water, a pot, a measuring cup, 1 package of **white alum** (you can buy alum in a supermarket), a spoon, a bowl, a magnifying glass, and a small hammer.

1. Put 16 ounces (500 milliliters) of water into the pot.

2. Add about 5 ounces (142 grams) of alum to the water.

3. Heat the water and stir it until the alum dissolves. Do not let the water boil.

4. After the alum dissolves, add a little more and stir again. Continue to do this until the alum will no longer dissolve.

5. Remove the pot from the heat and pour the water and alum mixture into an uncovered bowl.

6. Put the bowl aside for a few days. Soon you will see small alum crystals beginning to form in the bowl.

7. When the crystals get a little bigger, take them out of the water and dry them.

8. Examine the crystals' shapes with a magnifying glass.

9. Crush the crystals with a small hammer. Then, examine the crushed pieces with the magnifying glass. You should find that each of the crushed pieces has the same shape as the larger crystals.

GALENA.

PROPERTIES OF MINERALS

Some properties of minerals are **physical**. These are characteristics that we can see and test using simple methods. Other characteristics are **chemical**. The chemical composition of a mineral tells us what **element** or elements the mineral is made up of. (An element is any of more than one hundred basic substances that cannot be broken down into anything other than smaller pieces of itself.)

Chemical composition is shown using scientific symbols. Some minerals are made of a single element, like **sulfur**. Its scientific symbol is S. Other minerals are made up of more than one element, like **galena**, which is a combination of sulfur (S) and **lead** (Pb). The symbol for galena is PbS.

The physical properties of minerals are **color, luster, cleavage, streak, hardness,** and **specific gravity**.

Color

Sulfur, for example, is yellow, pyrite is gold, and **graphite** is black. But color alone is not a reliable clue in identifying a mineral because different minerals often have the same color, and some minerals come in more than one color. **Quartz**, for example, is sometimes purple, and the same is true of fluorite; using color alone, you would not be able to tell one from the other.

Luster

Luster refers to how shiny a mineral is. Some minerals, like **copper** and **zinc**, have a metallic luster. Others, like **diamond**, **asbestos,** and talc, have a nonmetallic luster. Some of the many words used to describe a mineral's nonmetallic luster are **glassy**, **dull**, **silky**, **earthy**, **waxy**, and **pearly**.

Do Your Own Streak Tests

Streak tests enable you to see how different minerals make different colored streaks.

You will need: an assortment of minerals (for example, malachite, pyrite, fluorite, hematite, quartz, or calcite), either collected from nature or purchased from a hobby shop, and an unglazed ceramic tile.

Rub the edge of each mineral along the ceramic tile. Compare the colors of the different streaks with the colors of the minerals that you made the streaks with.

Do Your Own Scratch Tests

Scratch tests help scientists determine the hardness of a mineral. A mineral's hardness refers to how well it resists being scratched.

You will need: a sharpened pencil, a penny, a piece of sandpaper, an aluminum pot, and a steel file.

1. Try to scratch each of the listed items with your fingernail. You will find that you can make a scratch mark only on the pencil point. Pencil points are made of the mineral graphite, which is very soft.

2. Try to scratch each of the items listed with one another. (Keep in mind that the penny is made of the mineral copper, the sand of the sandpaper is mostly quartz, and the steel in the file contains iron and manganese.) You will be able to compare the hardness of the different minerals by seeing which items make scratches on the others.

Cleavage

Cleavage describes the way in which a mineral splits when struck. This natural splitting usually follows the pattern of the mineral's crystal shape. **Beryl**, for example, has a **hexagonal** (six-sided) crystal structure. If you broke a chunk of beryl, the pieces would split along the lines of a hexagon. Galena is cubic, so it splits along the lines of a cube, and **mica** always splits into sheets. Not every mineral has neat cleavage when broken. When a mineral does not split neatly, it is said to have **fracture**.

Streak

When a mineral is rubbed across a piece of unglazed porcelain it leaves a colored powder. This color is known as the mineral's streak.

Sometimes a mineral's streak is the same color as the mineral, and sometimes it is not. For example, **malachite** is a green mineral that makes a green streak, and

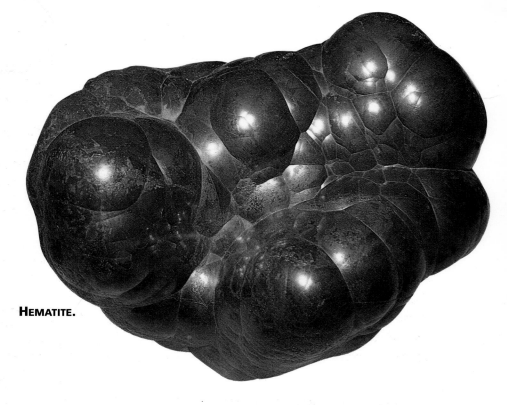

HEMATITE.

sulfur is a yellow mineral that makes a yellow streak. But **hematite**, a mineral that can be either black or red, always makes a red streak. Fluorite's streak is always white, although fluorite is found in various colors, including green, blue, purple, and yellow.

Hardness

A mineral's hardness refers to how well it resists scratching. To test hardness, scientists refer to a system designed by the German geologist **Friedrich Mohs**. The **Mohs' scale** ranges from 1 to 10; each number

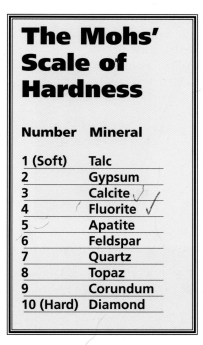

The Mohs' Scale of Hardness

Number	Mineral
1 (Soft)	Talc
2	Gypsum
3	Calcite
4	Fluorite
5	Apatite
6	Feldspar
7	Quartz
8	Topaz
9	Corundum
10 (Hard)	Diamond

Scratching Tools

The number next to each tool listed at right indicates the hardness of the mineral that the tool can scratch. For example, a penny can scratch calcite or any other mineral that has a hardness of 3 on the Mohs' scale. Because a tool can also scratch a mineral with a number on the scale that is lower than that of the tool, a penny can also scratch gypsum (2) and talc (1), but not fluorite (4).

Tool	Number of Hardness
Fingernail	2
Penny	3
Glass	5.5
Knife blade	5.5
Streak plate	6
Steel file	6.5

represents a specific mineral. Number 1, talc, is the softest of all minerals and is easily scratched. Number 10, diamond, is the hardest. A mineral of any given number can scratch another mineral of the same hardness or a mineral of a lesser hardness. Thus, only a diamond can scratch another diamond.

DIAMOND IS THE EARTH'S HARDEST MINERAL.

Specific Gravity

A mineral's specific gravity is its weight as compared to the weight of an equal volume of water. Corundum, for example, is four times as heavy as water. Its specific gravity is therefore 4. Diamond is just a little more than three-and-a-half times the weight of water; diamond's specific gravity is 3.52.

Many Colored Flames

To help them identify minerals, scientists use certain kinds of tests. One such test is the flame test. When a bit of powdered mineral is exposed to a flame, the flame will turn a certain color. The color the flame turns depends on the kinds of metals the mineral contains. Minerals containing copper, for example, will make a flame turn blue. **Strontium** will make a flame turn bright red.

Minerals that Glow

Ultraviolet light is a type of light that our eyes cannot detect. Some minerals absorb this light. Then, after the ultraviolet light has been cut off, these minerals give off the light they have absorbed. As the minerals give off this light, they glow in brilliant colors. Minerals that do this are called **fluorescent** minerals.

ABOVE, LEFT: THIS PIECE OF CALCITE IS SEEN HERE BEFORE BEING EXPOSED TO ULTRAVIOLET LIGHT. ABOVE, RIGHT: CALCITE, AFTER BEING EXPOSED TO ULTRAVIOLET LIGHT, GLOWS IN THE DARK AS IT RELEASES SOME OF THE ENERGY IT HAS ABSORBED.

Minerals that Release Energy

Some minerals release **radioactive energy**. This kind of energy cannot be seen, heard, or felt, but it can be recorded using an instrument called a **Geiger counter**. When a Geiger counter is placed near a radioactive mineral, the energy released will cause a needle on the instrument to move. Geiger counters are often used by prospectors mining for such metals as **uranium** and **thorium**, which are often radioactive.

ABOVE: THE GEIGER COUNTER WAS DEVELOPED AROUND 1911 BY GERMAN PHYSICIST HANS GEIGER AND HIS COLLEAGUE ERNEST RUTHERFORD. IT IDENTIFIES RADIOACTIVE MINERALS. BELOW: MUSCOVITE, SEEN HERE, IS A FORM OF MICA. BOTTOM: MAGNETITE.

SAMPLING THE MINERAL KINGDOM

Over two thousand kinds of minerals exist. Aside from the physical and chemical characteristics that allow us to identify them, many minerals have their own special traits that set them apart from others.

Magnetite

Magnetite is a black metallic mineral that got its name because it can be picked up by a magnet. One variety of magnetite, called **lodestone**, is itself a natural magnet that can pick up bits of iron and steel.

Mica

Mica is the name of a family of minerals. Mica's luster ranges from pearly to glassy, and its various colors include black, brown, gray, colorless, pale purple, and rose. All micas are famous for their cleavage. When mica breaks, it separates into sheets that are sometimes thinner than paper. Today, mica is used frequently in the manufacture of electronic equipment and eye makeup.

The Many Uses of Quartz

Quartz is one of the most common minerals of the earth, and one of the most widely used. In its pure form it is a colorless, glassy mineral that is sometimes called **rock crystal**. (The word *crystal* comes from the Greek word *kryos*, which means "icy cold." The ancient Greeks believed that quartz crystals were made of water so frozen that it would never thaw out.)

Sometimes, when pure quartz is forming in the earth, other minerals mix with it, giv- ing it a certain color. For example, the presence of iron turns quartz purple. We call purple quartz **amethyst**. Manganese turns quartz pink. Pink quartz is called **rose quartz**. Other kinds of quartz include **smoky quartz, milky quartz, citrine, tiger's-eye, agate, jasper,** and **carnelian**.

Many varieties of quartz are popular gemstones used in making jewelry. Quartz in its pure form is used to make glass, sandpaper, lenses, and watch faces. When cut at a certain angle, quartz gives off a slight electrical charge. This trait makes quartz a useful material in the manufacture of radio, television, and radar equipment, as well as clocks and computers.

THERE ARE MANY VARIETIES OF QUARTZ, INCLUDING AGATE (ABOVE), AMETHYST (ABOVE, MIDDLE), AND ROSE QUARTZ (ABOVE, FAR RIGHT).

CALCITE.

Calcite

Calcite is a glassy mineral that is usually colorless or white, but sometimes gray, red, green, or blue. Calcite is used in making cement and other building materials and has two special traits. First, it is the only mineral that bubbles when acid is dropped on it. This "acid test" is a sure way to identify this mineral. Second, if you look at an image through a colorless piece of calcite, the image will appear double.

Native Mercury

Native mercury is the only metal that is a liquid at room temperature. In liquid form, it is a silvery, metallic mineral that is sometimes called **quicksilver**. Combined with sulfur, it forms the bright red mineral **cinnabar**. Mercury is used in medicine and in the manufacture of thermometers and other medical instruments.

Staurolite

Staurolite is a glassy mineral that is brown to black in color. It usually forms twin crystals that intersect each other. Sometimes the crystals intersect at right angles to each other, forming a natural cross. These are known as **fairy crosses**. In areas where fairy crosses are found, local people and shop owners often collect them to sell to tourists.

ABOVE, RIGHT: THIS BEAUTIFUL EXAMPLE OF MALACHITE COMES FROM RUSSIA, IN THE FORMER SOVIET UNION. FAR RIGHT: GOLD IS ONE OF THE MOST TREASURED MINERALS; HERE A VEIN OF THE PRECIOUS YELLOW METAL RUNS THROUGH A CHUNK OF QUARTZ.

Malachite and Azurite

Malachite is a green and azurite a blue mineral that are often found together in

beautiful, naturally occurring swirl patterns. Both minerals are popular in the making of jewelry, vases, statuettes, and other pieces of art. Sometimes these two minerals are found in the shape of small round balls clustered together like a bunch of grapes.

Stretchy Metal

Gold is the most easily worked of all metals. One ounce (28 grams) of gold can be worked into a single wire a mile (1.6 kilometers) long. Metals that can be stretched out in this way are said to be **ductile** metals.

Minerals and the Products We Make from Them

Mineral	Product
Apatite	Fertilizer
Calcite	Cement, other building materials
Copper	Wire, pennies
Fluorite	Toothpaste
Feldspar	Porcelain ceramics, dishes
Graphite	Pencils
Gypsum	Plaster, cement, other building materials
Halite	Table salt, de-icing salt
Mica	Electronics, eye makeup
Native Mercury	Thermometers, other medical instruments
Quartz	Watches and clocks, computers, electronics, sandpaper, glass
Talc	Bath powder, cosmetics

CHAPTER TWO

ROCKS

LIMESTONE IS EASILY ERODED BY THE PASSAGE OF WATER, WHICH IS WHY SO MANY CAVES ARE HOLLOWED-OUT LIMESTONE FORMATIONS. HERE, IN THE BURREN, COUNTY CLARE, IRELAND, A BED OF LIMESTONE HAS BEEN SHAPED INTO THESE FANTASTIC SHAPES BY THE ELEMENTS.

The Three Classes of Rocks

All rocks belong to one of these three categories:

Igneous

Formed when molten rock from the Earth's mantle, called magma, cools.

Sedimentary

Formed when layers of ground-up rock particles, called sediment, harden.

Metamorphic

Formed when extreme heat or pressure from the earth changes one kind of rock into another.

WHERE DO ROCKS COME FROM?

Rocks are a combination of two or more minerals. Some rocks, such as limestone, are nearly all one mineral. Limestone is composed almost entirely of **calcite**. Other rocks, like granite, are made up of several different minerals. Granite is made up of feldspar, quartz, and mica. Unlike minerals, rocks can stretch uninterrupted for hundreds of miles across the Earth's crust.

There are three main categories of rock: **igneous**, **sedimentary**, and **metamorphic**.

Igneous

Igneous rocks are formed when magma from the Earth's mantle cools. Sometimes the magma enters cracks in the crust and cools there, underground. Rocks that form in this way are called **intrusive** igneous rocks. At other times the magma escapes onto the surface of the Earth as lava, which eventually hardens. Rocks formed in this way are called **extrusive** igneous rocks.

GRANITE.

Sedimentary

Powerful natural forces such as extreme cold or heat, high winds, and the movement of water and glaciers often grind up minerals and rocks. The fragments are then washed away by rain and rivers. As these fragments settle, they form layers, called **sediments**. Sediments that harden form sedimentary rock. If you look at sedimentary rocks, you can see different colored layers in them. The different colors come from the different kinds of rock and mineral fragments that formed the various sediments.

A Bowl of Sediments

To help you understand how sediments are deposited in nature, try the following experiment.

You will need: a handful of soil, a clear glass bowl, water, and a spoon.

1. Put the soil into the bowl. Then fill the bowl the rest of the way with water.

2. Stir the water with a spoon until the soil and water mix together.

3. Let the bowl sit for a few minutes. You will find that after the water stops moving, it separates the soil into different layers. Heavier particles in the soil, like pebbles, sink to the bottom. The lightest particles remain on top, while other layers form in between. This is similar to the way sedimentary rocks are formed.

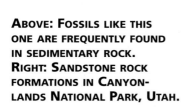

ABOVE: FOSSILS LIKE THIS ONE ARE FREQUENTLY FOUND IN SEDIMENTARY ROCK. RIGHT: SANDSTONE ROCK FORMATIONS IN CANYONLANDS NATIONAL PARK, UTAH.

Secrets in the Sediments

All around the world, fossils and **artifacts** (items made by people) can be found hidden inside the sediments of the earth. Sometimes these items are found in sedimentary rock, and sometimes they are found in softer sediments beneath the soil. Layers of soil are sometimes called **strata**. Archaeologists study the strata to figure out which artifacts and fossils are older or younger than others. This way of dating in archaeology is called **stratigraphy**. The idea behind stratigraphy is that sediments are laid down one on top of the other over time, with the oldest layers having been laid down first. As the archaeologist digs into the ground, the layers go from young to old. A fossil or artifact found in a layer deep within the ground will date to an earlier period of time than a fossil or artifact found in a layer above it.

FOSSILS: MEMENTOS OF THE LIVING PAST

Sometimes, when erosion wears away sedimentary rock, scenes from the past begin to emerge. The shapes of plants and animals, many now extinct, are revealed along with footprints, shells, teeth, and bones. These things buried in the rock are **fossils**, evidence of living organisms from long ago. Compared to the number of organisms that have existed on Earth since the planet was first formed, the number of organisms that have fossilized is very small.

Metamorphic

Metamorphic rock is rock that at one time used to be another kind of rock. Schist, for example, was once slate, which in turn was at one time the sedimentary rock shale. Metamorphic rock is created when extreme heat or pressure from the Earth changes the rock into a completely different form.

TOP: MARBLE IS A METAMORPHIC ROCK THAT IS VERY HARD DUE TO THE EXTREME PRESSURE THAT GOES INTO ITS CREATION. ABOVE: THIS IS THE OLDEST KNOWN FOSSIL OF A BIRD; IT DATES FROM THE LATE JURASSIC AND WAS FOUND IN SEDIMENTARY ROCK IN GERMANY.

Fossils form in several different ways. Sometimes the body of a plant or animal will be pressed into the earth so that it leaves an imprint. The body of the plant or animal decays, but the image of the organism embedded in the rock endures. At other times, particles of mud, sand, and various minerals fill in the cells of the organism as the organism itself decays, leaving behind a stone **replica**, or copy, of the organism. Usually this only happens with certain (usually the most durable) parts of the organism: teeth or bones, for example. A dinosaur bone isn't really a bone; rather, it is the fossilized remains of what used to be bone tissue.

Fossils form only in sedimentary rock. Because of the way igneous and metamorphic rocks are formed, an organism would be destroyed, either by heat or pressure, before it had a chance to fossilize.

Exploring Soil

Soil is formed when erosion breaks down rocks. These rock particles, mixed with decayed vegetable and animal material (called **humus**), make soil. You can see for yourself some of the different components in soil.

You will need: a tablespoon of soil, a sheet of white, unlined paper, and a magnifying glass.

1. Spread the soil on the sheet of paper.

2. Use the magnifying glass to examine the different parts, or components, of the soil.

In your soil sample, you may find particles of quartz, mica, and other minerals; the brown or black substance known as humus; pebbles; and clay. If you take two soil samples from two different places, chances are you will find the particles of each sample to be different.

THESE ARE THE FOSSILIZED SHELLS OF **AMMONITES**, EXTINCT SEA CREATURES ABUNDANT DURING THE MESOZOIC. LIKE MANY FOSSILS, THEY WERE PRESERVED OVER THE AGES IN SEDIMENTARY ROCK.

ROCKS IN OUR BACKYARD

The next time you are taking a walk or doing some other activity outside, pick up a rock and look closely at it. You may find that it looks a lot like the kinds of rocks used to build your school or local library. Or it may have the feel and texture of the walkway leading to your house or building. Many kinds of rocks are commonly used in the building industry. These rocks form the foundations of our cities and our homes.

GRANITE IS A DURABLE AND READILY AVAILABLE BUILDING MATERIAL. IT CAN ALSO BE QUITE BEAUTIFUL, LIKE THIS PIECE OF BIOTITE GRANITE. (BIOTITE IS A BLACK OR DARK GREEN FORM OF MICA.)

Granite

Granite is one of the most popular rocks used in the building industry because it is very strong and durable. An intrusive igneous rock, granite forms deep within the Earth's crust. Large quartz particles and mica flakes embedded in feldspar give granite its colorful, mottled appearance. Granite sometimes changes into the metamorphic rock **gneiss**, which is also a strong building stone.

Slate

Slate is a metamorphic rock. It is durable, fire-resistant, and can be split easily into sheets. For these reasons slate is an excellent material for making roofs, chalkboards, and walkways for yards and gardens.

THIS PICTURE SHOWS HOW SLATE NATURALLY BREAKS INTO FLAT SHEETS.

A Close Look at Sand

This experiment demonstrates that sand is made up of crushed rocks and minerals.

You will need: a tablespoon of sand, a sheet of white, unlined paper, and a magnifying glass.

1. Spread the sand on the sheet of paper.

2. Use the magnifying glass to examine the sand particles.

The most common mineral in sand is quartz. As you look carefully at the sand on the paper, you will see that it contains a great number of tiny quartz crystals, which look like shiny glass particles.

MARBLE.

Limestone

Limestone is another important building stone. It is a sedimentary rock formed mostly of the mineral calcite. Like calcite, limestone bubbles when acid is placed on it.

Because limestone dissolves easily in liquid, it often forms thick mud beneath the sea. Sea animals like clams and corals use these muds to help build their skeletons and shells. When the animals die, their skeletons and shells return to the muds, where everything is cemented together. For this reason, limestone cliffs and mountains that have been pushed up from the earth's crust often contain fossils of sea animals.

Marble

Under the right conditions, limestone transforms into the metamorphic rock marble. Marble, which is often very colorful, is prized by artists and builders for its beauty. Sometimes it is pure white, sometimes it has swirls and streaks, and sometimes it is tinged with color, such as pink or green. Slabs of marble are often used to decorate the insides and outsides of buildings. The fine white variety has also been used for some of the most famous sculptures in the world.

Rusty Rocks

Have you ever looked at a rock and found that it appeared to have rust on it? To find out why this is so, try this experiment.

You will need: a saucer, a tablespoon, water, vinegar, an iron nail, and a glass.

1. On the saucer, combine about two tablespoons of water and two or three drops of vinegar.

2. Place the nail in the mixture of vinegar and water.

3. Place the glass upside down over the nail. The glass will keep the nail trapped in moist air.

4. Put the experiment aside for a few hours. When you return, you will find that the nail has begun to rust.

Water and moist air will always cause iron to rust; in this experiment, the acid in the vinegar helps to speed the process up. Some rocks are made of minerals that contain iron. Water and moist air will sometimes cause the iron in rocks to rust, which is why these rocks sometimes have a rusty appearance.

Sandstone

Sandstone is a sedimentary rock formed from sand, so it feels gritty when you touch it. Although sand is made up mostly of quartz, sandstone can also have other minerals in it, like mica, feldspar, and magnetite. Much of the brownstone used to make the famous brownstone homes of New York City is a kind of sandstone.

PUMICE.

Pumice and Obsidian

Pumice and obsidian are examples of extrusive igneous rocks. Both are formed from lava, yet they look very different. Pumice is formed from slow-cooling lava. It is a gray, spongelike rock that is so light it floats on water. Because of its rough texture, pumice is sold in stores as a natural material that is used to smooth rough, dry skin. Obsidian is formed when lava cools quickly. It is a natural glass that is usually black, although sometimes brown or red.

OBSIDIAN.

When obsidian breaks, its edges are very sharp. In the past, in various parts of the world, obsidian was used to make tools, weapons, and mirrors.

LIKE THESE BUILDINGS IN NEW YORK CITY, BUILDINGS IN CITIES AND TOWNS ACROSS THE WORLD ARE MADE USING THE ROCKS AND MINERALS OF THE EARTH'S CRUST.

SOMETIMES BUILDINGS HAVE DECORATIVE CARVINGS (LIKE THESE SANDSTONE FIGURES) SCULPTED INTO THEIR FACADES.

Rocks and What We Humans Use Them For

Rock	What It's Used For
Granite	Building stones
Limestone	Building stones
Marble	Decorating walls, floors, and stairways of buildings; sculpture
Pumice	Material for smoothing rough skin
Sandstone	Building stones
Slate	Chalkboards, roofing tiles, walkways

CHAPTER THREE

GEMS

THE FAMOUS HOPE DIAMOND IN THE MIDDLE OF AN EXTRAV-
AGANT SETTING THAT HIGHLIGHTS THE BLUE STONE'S BEAUTY.

The Hope Diamond

In 1642 a large, deep blue diamond was brought from India to France and was eventually sold to **King Louis XIV** in 1668. In France it was cut into a gem that weighed over 67 **carats** (see page 34). This diamond was seized from French royalty during the French Revolution in 1792 and then disappeared. A diamond that was believed to be part of this French one appeared in 1830 in London, and was sold to **Sir Henry Thomas Hope**. Known as the Hope Diamond, it weighs 44.5 carats and sits today in the Smithsonian Institution in Washington, D.C.

TREASURES OF THE EARTH

For as far back as we can tell, humans have been fascinated by the idea of discovering hidden treasure. The hope of finding measureless wealth in money or gems has been the cause of many wars, murders, thefts, and adventurous journeys around the world. But what are gems, and what makes them so precious?

A gem may be a diamond, a pearl, or any other natural nonliving object that is considered to have value. Usually, something is considered valuable when it is rare or difficult to find.

Gems are most often used in making jewelry and in decorating personal items, although some gems are carved into charms and amulets. A gem used for adornment must first be cut into a shape that is pleasing to look at. This is done by a person called a **lapidary**.

WHEN CERTAIN MINERALS THAT ARE VALUED FOR THEIR BEAUTY AND DURABILITY ARE CUT AND POLISHED, LIKE THIS SAPPHIRE, THEY ARE CALLED GEMS.

GEMS FROM THE LAND

Some gems are rocks, like dark blue **lapis luzuli** and glassy obsidian. Most often, though, gems are minerals. When the mineral beryl, for example, is a light blue-green color, it is known as **aquamarine**. When it is a rich, dark green, it is called an **emerald**. Different colors of the mineral **corundum** form the striking red **ruby** and the deep blue **sapphire**. The mineral **tourmaline** comes in almost every color imaginable, and sometimes it occurs in a combination of colors. Thus, a ring made with tourmaline may have a stone that is half green and half red.

To be considered a gemstone, a mineral must have certain qualities: it must be beautiful, rare, and durable, and it must reflect light in a spectacular way. (This last quality is known as the gem's **brilliance**.) Of all the mineral gems, diamond is unsurpassed in these qualities and is therefore considered to be the most valuable of all gems. Besides the clear variety, diamonds also occur in other colors, such as red, green, blue, and yellow.

Diamonds, sapphires, rubies, and emeralds are the most precious of all the gemstones. Their weight is measured in **carats** rather than grams or ounces

The Star of India and the DeLong Star Ruby

Two of the most magnificent "star" gems in the world are the Star of India and the DeLong Star Ruby. "Stars" are formed in gems when the mineral **rutile** is present as the mineral is forming in the Earth. When the gem is cut in a dome shape, the light reflecting off the rutile crystals makes it look like there is a star shining in the center of the gem.

The Star of India was mined in Sri Lanka over three hundred years ago. It weighs 563 carats (see page 34) and is the largest blue star sapphire known in the world today. The DeLong Star Ruby, mined in Burma, weighs 100 carats. Both the DeLong Star Ruby and the Star of India are on display at the American Museum of Natural History in New York City.

THIS IS WHAT AN UNPOLISHED, NEWLY MINED RUBY LOOKS LIKE.

EMERALD CRYSTALS.

THIS TOURMALINE IS NESTLED IN A BED OF WHITE QUARTZ.

Gemstone of the Month

Since ancient times, people all over the world have valued gemstones. In many places, certain gems were believed to have magical powers that would bring the wearer good fortune or protection from harm. Some of these were connected to a particular month of the year. The practice of wearing a gemstone connected to the month a person was born probably did not begin until the eighteenth century, in Poland. Today, wearing a birthstone is common throughout the world.

(a carat is equivalent to 200 milligrams). Other mineral gems, like **opal** and **topaz**, though still valuable, are considered less precious. Still others, like **turquoise** and **jadeite**, are actually quite common.

Some gems found in the earth are not rocks or minerals, but fossils. **Amber** is a gem, but it is also a fossil because it is the hardened sap from trees that lived

Birthstones

LIKE THESE CLASS RINGS, MOST BIRTHSTONE JEWELRY IS MADE USING SYNTHETIC GEMSTONES.

Month	Birthstone	Month	Birthstone
January	Garnet	July	Ruby
February	Amethyst	August	Peridot or Sardonyx
March	Aquamarine or Bloodstone	September	Sapphire
April	Diamond	October	Opal or Tourmaline
May	Emerald	November	Topaz or Citrine
June	Pearl or Alexandrite	December	Turquoise or Zircon

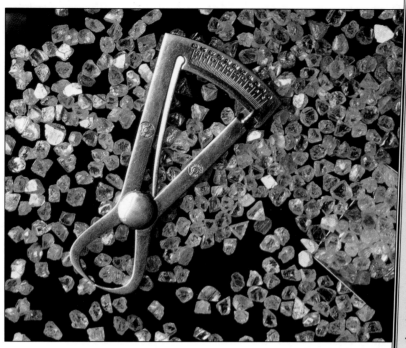

DIAMONDS LOOK LIKE LITTLE ROUGH-EDGED CHUNKS OF GLASS BEFORE BEING CUT AND POLISHED; THE INSTRUMENTS SHOWN IN THIS PICTURE ARE FOR SCOOPING AND MEASURING THE DIAMONDS.

The Same, Yet Different

Diamond and graphite are both made of a single element: carbon. Yet diamond is a precious gem and graphite is common pencil "lead." The difference between the two minerals is in the way their atoms are arranged. All the elements of the earth are made up of particles called atoms, but sometimes the atoms in an element are arranged one way, sometimes another. When atoms of carbon are arranged in layers, they form the mineral graphite. When they are clustered together in a strong bond, they form diamond.

millions of years ago. Petrified wood is another kind of fossil that is used as a gem. Petrified wood is formed when the cells of a tree's trunk are replaced over time by minerals. A third type of fossil gem is **jet**, a kind of coal (which is fossilized plant material) that can be shined to a rich luster.

GEMS BENEATH THE WATER

Some gems do not come from the earth's crust, but are formed in rivers and seas. **Cameos**, for example,

MOLLUSK SHELLS THAT ARE USED FOR CAMEOS LIKE THIS ONE ARE DURABLE, BEAUTIFUL, AND EASY TO CARVE.

are handmade gems created by carving the shells of certain mollusks. Another water gem is **coral,** which is created by tiny animals called **coral polyps.** Coral polyps release calcite from their bodies to make exterior skeletons for themselves. As they form, these skeletons, or corals, branch out like tree limbs. Coral can be red, white, black, orange, pink, or blue.

Mother-of-Pearl

Nacre, the material made by mollusks that forms pearls, is the same material that lines the inside of the animals' shells. This lining is called mother-of-pearl. It is often used to decorate furniture, jewelry boxes, musical instruments, and other items made of wood.

HUMANS PRIZE PEARLS HIGHLY, BUT TO THE OYSTERS THAT CREATE THESE BEAUTIFUL LITTLE GLOBES, PEARLS ARE FORMED TO SOOTHE IRRITATIONS.

Although shell and coral are popular gem materials, the most valuable of water gems is the pearl. When a grain of sand or other particle enters the shell of a mollusk, it will begin to irritate the animal's flesh. The mollusk tries to protect itself by coating the particle with layers of **nacre**, the same material its shell is made of. The result is a smooth, shimmering pearl that is usually white, but can sometimes be black, pink, or yellow.

CULTURED PEARLS (LIKE THE ONES IN THIS NECKLACE) ARE DIFFICULT TO TELL FROM THEIR NATURALLY OCCURRING COUNTERPARTS.

Cultured Pearls

Natural pearls have always been rare and difficult to find. To get a few high-quality pearls, it is necessary to open thousands of mollusks. At the turn of the century in Japan, two men figured out a way to "grow" pearls with the help of mollusks. By inserting a mother-of-pearl bead into a mollusk, the men found that the animal would respond just as it would if a grain of sand or other particle had entered its shell: it would coat the bead with nacre and form a pearl. Pearls formed in this way are called cultured pearls.

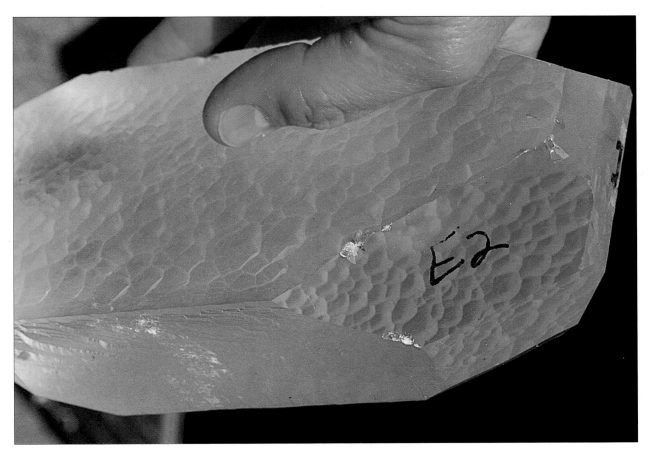

SYNTHETIC GEMSTONES, LIKE THIS CHUNK OF QUARTZ, ARE MADE IN THE LABORATORY.

People-Made Gemstones

Sometimes jewelry is made with **synthetic** gemstones. These are gemstones that have been grown in a laboratory rather than in nature. Synthetic gemstones are more affordable than real gemstones and, if well made, are difficult to distinguish from their naturally occurring cousins.

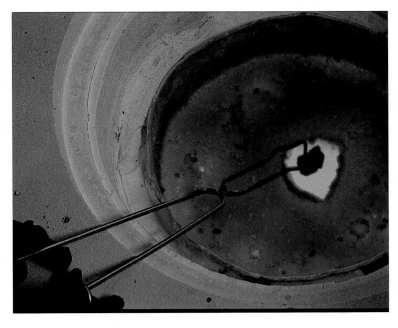

ONE OF THE FIRST STEPS IN MAKING A SYNTHETIC EMERALD, A SMALL CHUNK OF NATURAL EMERALD IS INSERTED INTO A "FURNACE" FILLED WITH MAGMA, WHERE IT "GROWS" INTO A LARGER EMERALD.

CHAPTER FOUR

CAVES AND CAVERNS: UNDERGROUND ROOMS OF STONE

CARLSBAD CAVERNS, NEW MEXICO, IS AN ENORMOUS UNDERGROUND NATIONAL PARK THAT HAS BEEN ONLY PARTLY EXPLORED.

ROOMS AND TUNNELS BENEATH THE EARTH

All across the Earth, openings in the crust serve as entrances to spectacular underground chambers called **caves** or **caverns**. Mazes of tunnels and rooms in any one cave may run for miles beneath the ground, twisting and turning, rising toward the surface or plunging deeper into the Earth. The caves may be so narrow that a person has to crawl on his or her belly to pass or so vast that they resemble airplane hangars.

Caves are cool, dark places that are home to a variety of plants and animals. Of course, caves are also good places to find fascinating mineral and rock formations. Today, many caves are open to the public to visit. In North America, many caves are protected by government institutions, such as the National Park Service in the United States and Parks Canada in Canada.

Carlsbad Caverns

Carlsbad Caverns in New Mexico is one of the most magnificent caves in the world. Inside its huge rooms are all kinds of interesting formations, including a great variety of **stalactites** and **stalagmites** (see page 42). Some of these formations have names that describe what they resemble: the Frozen Waterfall, the Whale's Mouth, the Baby Hippo, the Veiled Statue, and the King's Draperies. One room in the cave, called the Big Room, is the largest underground cavern known in the world today. Its floor space has the same area as fourteen football fields and its ceiling reaches 255 feet (78.5 meters) at its highest point.

Bubbling Limestone

Most caves in the world are made of the sedimentary rock limestone. Limestone is made mostly of the mineral calcite, which bubbles when cold acid is placed on it. To see for yourself, try this experiment.

You will need: a steel file, a piece of limestone, and vinegar (a form of acid).

1. Using the steel file, scrape the piece of limestone until you have a small amount of limestone powder.

2. Place a few drops of vinegar on the limestone and watch the mixture fizz.

KINDS OF CAVES

Caves come in a variety of types, although most of the world's caves are limestone. Because limestone dissolves easily in liquid, hundreds of thousands of years of rainwater seeping through the soil has dissolved the rock in many places across the Earth, forming limestone caves. **Gypsum** is another easily dissolved mineral that forms caves in this way, although gypsum caves are not as big as limestone caves. Often, gypsum crystals are found growing in limestone caves.

Some caves are formed from sandstone, a rock that is easily eroded by wind and rain. Sandstone caves are very shallow. Because they were often used by early peoples for shelter, they are also known as **cliff dwellings** or **rock shelters**.

Ice caves are caves found in areas with cold climates and high elevations. The rock outside of the cave insulates the rooms and keeps the ice inside from melting.

MANY CENTURIES AGO, EARLY PUEBLO PEOPLES OF THE SOUTHWEST LIVED IN CLIFF DWELLINGS. TODAY, VISITORS CAN WALK THROUGH THE RUINS OF SOME OF THESE VILLAGES, SUCH AS CLIFF PALACE (SHOWN HERE) IN MESA VERDE NATIONAL PARK, COLORADO.

LAVA TUBE AT CRATERS OF THE MOON NATIONAL MONUMENT, IDAHO.

Sea caves are found underwater. They are formed by the pressure of sea water battering the walls of cliffs over hundreds of thousands of years. The water erodes the rock, forming tunnels and rooms.

Another kind of cave, the **lava tube**, is the only cave that does not take a long time to form. A lava tube forms when a volcano erupts and rivers of lava flow down its side and around its base. As the lava cools around the volcano's base, the outside hardens and forms a crust. Inside, the hot molten rock continues to flow until it eventually drains out. What is left behind is the tubelike crust of hardened lava.

Visiting Caves in the Nineteenth Century

Some caves in the United States were open to tourists as early as 1825. At that time, guides led visitors through the unlighted rooms and corridors with torches, lanterns, and lamps. The visitors wore special clothes and had to crawl, crouch, and squeeze their way through the often narrow passageways. (In the twentieth century, the exploration of caves was made easier by the growth of technology; the practice came to be known as **spelunking**.)

USING LIGHTED HELMETS AND OTHER SPECIAL EQUIPMENT, SPELUNKERS SUCH AS THIS SQUEEZE THEIR WAY THROUGH SOME TIGHT SPACES.

WIND CAVE, SOUTH DAKOTA.

Wind Cave

In South Dakota in 1881, two brothers were out walking when they heard a loud whistling sound. They followed the sound and found a small opening that led to a cave. The whistling sound was made by wind coming from the opening. This is how Wind Cave got its name.

Wind Cave is well known for having some of the world's most beautiful **boxwork** (see page 43). Experts guess that the cave probably has about 55 miles (88 kilometers) of passageways, but only a few miles' worth have been discovered and explored so far.

NATURAL SCULPTURES

As you explore a cave, you may find fossils of shellfish and coral, naturally formed pools of water, and many beautiful kinds of rock formations growing on the walls, floors, and ceilings. Perhaps the most familiar of these formations are **stalactites** and **stalagmites**. Stalactites are caused by the dripping of water that seeps from the surface down into the cave. The water falls one drop at a time from the cave ceiling, sometimes carrying dissolved limestone with it. The water eventually evaporates, and any limestone that the water contained will leave behind a small bit of calcite on the cave ceiling. Over time, these small deposits build up and become an icicle-shaped stalactite that hangs from the ceiling.

If the drop of water falls from the ceiling and hits a flat surface on the cave floor, it may begin to form a stalagmite. Stalagmites, like stalactites, are formed when small amounts of calcite build up, except that stalagmites grow from the ground up. Some stalagmites, called **broomsticks**, are very straight and skinny. Sometimes a stalactite and a stalagmite meet in the middle and join together. This formation is called a **column**.

ABOVE: STALACTITES AND STALAGMITES. RIGHT: BIG SKYLIGHT CAVE AT EL MALPAIS NATIONAL MONUMENT, NEW MEXICO.

BOXWORK IN WIND CAVE,
SOUTH DAKOTA.

A formation similar to the stalactite and stalagmite is the strange and puzzling **helictite**. Helictites, too, are formed by drops of water that carry calcite, but helictites do not grow vertically. Instead, they twist and turn like plant roots.

Another interesting formation found in caves is **boxwork**. Boxwork looks like a fragile honeycomb covering parts of the walls or ceiling of the cave. It is actually formed by thin ribbons of calcite that crisscross each other. Boxwork is one of many kinds of cave formations that are both beautiful and exotic. Other formations include **popcorn**, **lily pads**, **cave pearls**, and delicate **gypsum flowers** and **selenite needles**.

Mammoth Cave

Kentucky's Mammoth Cave is a popular cave with an interesting history. Items found in the cave—like pottery, sandals, wooden bowls, and even a natural mummy—show that the cave was used long ago by early Native Americans living in the vicinity. Later, during the **War of 1812**, the cave became an important source of **nitrates**, chemicals that were essential to the manufacture of gunpowder.

Still later, in 1843, a doctor named **John Croghan** used Mammoth Cave in a radical medical experiment. The doctor believed that the steady temperature and high humidity of the cave air would be a good environment for the sick. So he built twelve cottages inside the cave for patients with **tuberculosis** (a potentially fatal disease that affects the lungs). Fifteen patients stayed in the cottages for several months but were not cured. In fact, records show that the patients were even sicker when they left the cave than they had been when they went in. Today, two of the cottages are still there for visitors to see.

ALTHOUGH THEY CAN FLY, BATS ARE NOT BIRDS—THEY ARE MAMMALS SIMILAR TO RODENTS. MOST ARE **NOCTURNAL** ANIMALS, WHICH MEANS THEY HUNT FOR FOOD AT NIGHT AND SLEEP DURING THE DAY. BATS OFTEN MAKE THEIR HOMES IN CAVES, WHERE THEY ARE SAFE FROM ALL THE **DIURNAL** ANIMALS (ANIMALS THAT ARE ACTIVE DURING THE DAY).

DRAPERY FORMATIONS HANG FROM THE CEILING IN THIS LIMESTONE CAVE IN MISSOURI.

Caves to Visit

There are hundreds of parks, open to the public, throughout the United States and Canada that feature spectacular caves. Visitors can take an underground tour with a professional guide along safe, well-lighted pathways. Some of the more popular caves are listed below.

Park	State or Province
Anemone Cave	Maine
Carlsbad Caverns National Park	New Mexico
Crystal Ice Caves	Idaho
Flowerpot Island (Georgian Bay Islands Park)	Ontario
Howe Caverns	New York
Jewel Cave National Monument	South Dakota
Lava Beds National Monument	California
Luray Caverns	Virginia
Mammoth Cave National Park	Kentucky
Nahanni Park	Northwest Territories
Oregon Caves National Monument	Oregon
Russell Cave National Monument	Alabama
Timpanogos Cave National Monument	Utah
Wind Cave National Park	South Dakota

CHAPTER FIVE

NATIONAL PARKS: OPEN-AIR GEOLOGIC MUSEUMS

LAND FOR THE PEOPLE

National parks in the United States and Canada feature a wide variety of terrains, including forests, deserts, caves, canyons, and many other natural wonders. Visiting these parks is a marvelous way to witness for yourself how natural forces have shaped the Earth's crust. As you wander through these places, you may even be able to recognize many of the rocks and minerals that form the landscape.

ABOVE: AN EARLY MORNING FOG RISES IN YOSEMITE NATIONAL PARK, CALIFORNIA. RIGHT: CANARY SPRING IN YELLOWSTONE NATIONAL PARK, WYOMING.

YELLOWSTONE

With its colorful wildlife, steaming geysers, and towering mountains, Yellowstone National Park (established in 1872 as a federally protected area in Wyoming and parts of Idaho and Montana) has some of the most beautiful natural scenery in the world. Because of its beauty, Yellowstone was established as a preserve and opened to the public to visit and enjoy. It was the first national park in the United States. The idea of setting aside land for the public's enjoyment was so successful that in 1916 Congress established the National Park Service to preserve the country's many wilderness areas and historic sites.

Canyon in a Jar

Canyons are great places to see the layer-cake look of sedimentary rock. The layers of rock form slowly over long periods of time, each layer containing different rock particles and minerals. The process of erosion exposes these different layers in cross section. The result looks like a "rock cake" of different colors and shades.

To re-create the various color combinations found in canyon walls, you can make a miniature "canyon" of your own.

You will need: a glass jar with a lid, spices (salt, brown sugar, black pepper, red pepper, oregano, powdered garlic), rice, corn flakes, and unpopped popcorn kernels.

1. Pour about ½ inch (1.3 centimeters) of brown sugar into the jar and shake the jar gently until the sugar forms a flat layer.

2. Over the sugar, add a layer of black pepper or one of the other items listed above.

3. Continue to form layers using the items listed until you have reached the top of the jar.

4. Screw the lid on the jar. You now have your own colorful "canyon wall."

BRYCE CANYON

Visitors to Bryce Canyon National Park in Utah will find rock formations in the shapes of domes, spires, bridges, arches, windows, walls, and even people in shades of red, pink, and white. These magnificent natural sculptures sit inside a horseshoe-shaped bowl that was carved into the Paunsaugunt Plateau by natural forces. The bowl, or canyon, is about two miles (3.2 kilometers) wide, three miles (4.8 kilometers) long, and one thousand feet (305 meters) deep.

Bryce Canyon is made of limestone, shale, and sandstone. The variety of colorful shades found in the rocks was caused by the presence of various minerals, such as hematite, that were present in the layers of sediment that were deposited. After these sedimentary rocks were formed, the shifting of the earth's plates caused the **plateau** to form. Erosion then chiseled the rock formations out of the plateau.

ANVIL ROCK IN BRYCE CANYON NATIONAL PARK, UTAH.

DEVIL'S TOWER

The drive to Devil's Tower National Monument in Wyoming takes the traveler over rolling hills with grassy slopes that are covered with cottonwood and yellow pines. Suddenly, as the traveler draws near, a single huge rock formation can be seen in the distance. It looks like the stump of a giant tree popping up out of the landscape. This is Devil's Tower.

Devil's Tower is actually the solid core of an underground volcano. About 60 million years ago, magma from the earth's mantle pushed into the crust. But the magma did not surface above the sedimentary rock it pushed into. It remained in the rock underneath the earth's surface. There, it slowly cooled and the molten magma became solid. As the sedimentary rock around it eroded, the solid core was exposed. This core, now called Devil's Tower, is 867 feet (264 meters) from base to top.

A Kiowa Legend

According to a story told by the Kiowa, Devil's Tower was formed when a young boy turned into a bear and tried to harm his seven sisters. The frightened girls ran for their lives while the bear chased them. Finally, the girls came upon the stump of a giant tree, which spoke to them, telling them to climb upon it. When they did, it began rising into the air and became today's Devil's Tower. Meanwhile, the sisters were taken up into the sky and were turned into the stars of the Big Dipper.

DEVIL'S TOWER NATIONAL MONUMENT, WYOMING.

BADLANDS

In the past, as French-Canadian trappers traveled across the grasslands of what is today South Dakota, they came across an area of land that was extremely difficult to cross. They described the area as "bad lands to travel over," and so the area became known as the Badlands.

Today, the region is Badlands National Park.

The place those early trappers found so difficult to cross is a place of carved canyons and sculpted peaks. It looks very different from the open grasslands that surround it. Badlands is composed mainly of sedimentary rock in which a treasure of fossils is buried. The oldest layer of rock is black shale from 65 million years ago. The other layers formed between 37 and 23 million years ago. The rock formations of the Badlands were created by years of erosion caused by the elements.

BADLANDS NATIONAL PARK, SOUTH DAKOTA.

TOP: PETRIFIED FOREST NATIONAL
PARK, ARIZONA. ABOVE: DAISIES
GROW NEAR A PIECE OF FOSSILIZED
WOOD IN PETRIFIED FOREST
NATIONAL PARK.

PETRIFIED FOREST

In the dry, almost desert landscape of northern Arizona, a forest of fallen trees (actually, they are just logs now) lies scattered about the grounds of Petrified Forest National Park. The logs are multicolored: purple, blue, red, brown, yellow, orange, green, and black. But these logs are no longer made of wood. They are fossilized, or **petrified**, logs, which means the wood has been replaced by minerals.

About 200 million years ago, a forest of living trees grew along a stream, perhaps a hundred miles (161 kilometers) from the present-day Petrified Forest. Over time, as the trees died of natural causes, some of them fell into the stream, which carried the logs away, later to be buried in mud and sand. Once buried, the wood was slowly replaced by minerals, mostly many different kinds of colored quartz. Finally, the process of erosion exposed the fossilized trees.

MORAINE LAKE IN BANFF NATIONAL PARK, CANADA.

BANFF NATIONAL PARK

Featuring many lakes, rivers, mountains, and valleys, Banff National Park, located in Alberta, is perhaps the most popular park in Canada. Noted for its incredible mountain scenery, the park is the oldest national park in Canada and was the forerunner of the country's national park system.

Among Banff's highlights are the turquoise-colored waters of Moraine Lake, which was referred to as the Goat's Looking Glass by the Native Americans of the region. Notably, Banff features a system of hot springs, which bubble down the slopes of Mount Sulphur. The water in these springs is heated deep in the Earth's crust and is impregnated with sulfur; the curative power of such springs was noted by Native Americans long before North America was colonized by Europeans.

National Parks to Visit

Listed below are a few of the hundreds of national parks and monuments in the United States and Canada.

Park	State or Province
Agate Fossil Beds National Monument	Nebraska
Banff National Park	Alberta
Bryce Canyon National Park	Utah
Cape Breton Highlands Park	Nova Scotia
Devil's Tower National Monument	Wyoming
Badlands National Park	South Dakota
Fundy Park	New Brunswick
Glacier National Park	Montana
Glacier Park	British Columbia
Grand Canyon National Park	Arizona
Grand Teton National Park	Wyoming
Hawaii Volcanoes National Park	Hawaii
La Maurice Park	Quebec
Mesa Verde National Park	Colorado
Petrified Forest National Park	Arizona
Pipestone National Monument	Minnesota
Riding Mountain Park	Manitoba
Yosemite National Park	California

THE WINTER SUN RISES OVER SNAKE RIVER IN GRAND TETON NATIONAL PARK, WYOMING.

GLACIER PARK

Located in the Selkirk Mountains in British Columbia, Glacier Park is nestled in the great northern bend of the Columbia River. Founded in 1886, this park is a magnificent place to see firsthand how the slow, steady passage of glaciers has changed the face of the planet over the millennia. From some peaks in Glacier Park it is possible to see the tracks of more than one hundred glaciers that have slowly threaded their way down the mountainsides. The mountainsides themselves are clothed in thick forest and the park is dotted throughout with stunning waterfalls that originate in the glaciers themselves.

CHAPTER SIX

FROM SPEAR POINTS TO SACRED PIPES

EARLY NATIVE AMERICANS MADE ARROWHEADS OUT OF VARIOUS ROCKS AND MINERALS, INCLUDING **CHERT**, OBSIDIAN, FLINT, AND QUARTZ.

WHEN ROCKS COULD MOVE

Native peoples of North America have many stories in which rocks and minerals play important roles. One story from the **Shasta** Indians of California tells how the people got obsidian to make arrowheads.

Long ago, the story goes, hunters had to use bark to make their arrowheads because they did not know where to find obsidian, which is a much harder material. Ground Squirrel, who alone knew where Obsidian Old Man lived,

agreed to try and get some of the obsidian.

Ground Squirrel went to Obsidian Old Man's home and complained of being sick. Hearing this, Obsidian Old Man went out to gather wood for a fire. While Obsidian Old Man was out, Ground Squirrel stole all the obsidian points in the house and brought them back to the people.

The Navajo of the Southwest have a story about how the sun and moon were created from slabs of quartz. First Man and First Woman wanted more light in the world,

so they cut two circles of quartz using flint tools. They decorated the sun circle with turquoise and the moon circle with white shell. Then, after blessing the two disks with the proper rituals, First Man and First Woman climbed to a mountaintop and hung the sun and moon in the sky.

The Lakota of the Plains have a story about how their people came to be. There was a fight between the ancient Lakota and the water monster Unktehi. Unktehi caused a great flood that filled the land.

TO MAKE THEIR SACRED PIPES, PLAINS INDIANS HAVE MINED PIPESTONE FOR CENTURIES. GEORGE CATLIN CAP-TURED THE SPIRIT OF THIS IMPORTANT ACTIVITY IN THIS PAINTING, *COTEAU DES PRAIRES* **(1836–1837).**

To save themselves, the people climbed to the tops of some hills. But the flood eventually covered the hills, too, and all the people were killed except for one beautiful girl. The blood of all the dead people came together in one big pool and hardened. It became the red rock **pipestone**.

Meanwhile, Eagle had saved the beautiful girl. He flew away with her to his home high on a mountain-top. Eagle and the Lakota girl married and had chil-dren. Over time, new gen-erations were born, filling the land with the Lakota people once again.

Today in Montana there is a quarry where pipe-stone, or **catlinite**, is found. This rock is used to make the sacred pipes smoked by the Lakota when they pray in the traditional manner.

THE SACRED PIPES OF THE PLAINS INDIANS HAVE TWO CONNECTING PIECES: A BOWL AND A STEM. THIS CATLINITE BOWL WAS MADE BY A LAKOTA ARTISAN.

MATERIALS FROM NATURE

Native Americans have long used rocks, minerals, and gems in a variety of ways. They used these materials in ceremonies and also in making such everyday items as tools, utensils, and ornaments.

Most of the items made for everyday use were finely crafted and beautifully decorated. Arrowheads, spearheads, and knives, for example, were made with great skill by many Native Americans from such mate-rials as obsidian, quartz, and flint. Some of the finest pottery in the world has been made by the **Pueblo**

"Soap"stone Carvings

For countless generations, the Inuit people of the Arctic have used soapstone to make carvings and household items. Soapstone has a great deal of talc in it, making it a soft rock that is easily carved. The talc also gives it a "soapy" feel. Using a bar of real soap, you can make carvings similar to the ones made of soapstone by Inuit artists.

You will need: a pocket knife, a bar of soap, a pencil, and a soft, dry cloth.

1. Using the pocket knife, scrape the top and underside of the bar of soap so that the imprinted brand name no longer shows.

2. Use the pencil to etch an outline of what you are going to carve. It may be an animal, a flower, a person, or anything else you want to sculpt. (The Inuit often make carvings of animals found in the Arctic.)

3. Carve the soap, using the etching as a guideline.

4. When your carving is complete, use the cloth to smooth its edges and polish it.

A CLAY BOWL FROM ACOMA PUEBLO.

peoples of the Southwest using natural clays. In the Arctic, the **Inuit** made oil lamps and pots of carved soapstone.

Paints for decorating items and people's bodies were made by crushing minerals like hematite, malachite, and azurite into powders and mixing them with liquid.

In the Southwest, the **Zuni** Indians are well known for their carved **fetishes**. Fetishes are small carvings that are usually in the form of animals and made from materials like turquoise, coral, jet, shell, or malachite. They represent the spirits of animals and natural forces, like wind and thunder. The power of the spirit represented by the fetish is thought to protect and help the owner.

Minerals are also used in the Southwest by the **Navajo** Indians during their healing ceremonies. During these ceremonies, a medicine man or woman uses different colored sands made from sandstone and mudstone, charcoal, cornmeal, crushed flowers, and plant pollen to make a sand painting. If made in the proper ritual way, a sand painting becomes very powerful. The patient then sits on the sand painting to absorb its curative power.

Figures Etched in Stone

All across North America, animals, spirit figures, and geometric shapes can be found carved into cliffs and rock faces. These etchings are called **petroglyphs** and were created by Native American artists over one thousand years ago.

PETROGLYPHS FROM NEWSPAPER ROCK, UTAH.

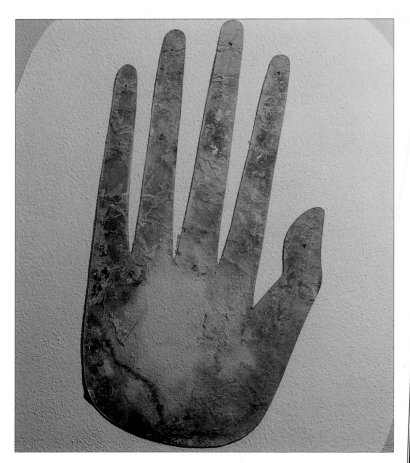

A MICA CUTOUT FROM HOPEWELL, OHIO.

Treasures of the Mound Builders

Long ago, Native Americans living in what is today called the Midwest had built a great and complex civilization. These early peoples are known today as the Mound Builders because of the large earthen mounds they made to bury their dead. Like peoples in many cultures, the Mound Builders placed items in the graves of their leaders and loved ones. At a site called Hopewell, Ohio, some of the items found in these burial mounds include copper jewelry, headdresses, axes, freshwater pearls, and finely made blades of obsidian, cutouts of hands, animals, and geometric shapes made from sheets of mica. Many of these items were made over fifteen hundred years ago.

Today, sand paintings, fetishes, and pipes are still used by Native American peoples for religious purposes. The practice of creating beautiful everyday objects continues as well, but now many of these items are made as art objects. The Inuit, for example, still carve soapstone. Many Inuit carvers today make their livings as artists who sell their carvings to collectors. The same is true of Pueblo pottery. And more and more Native American artists today are

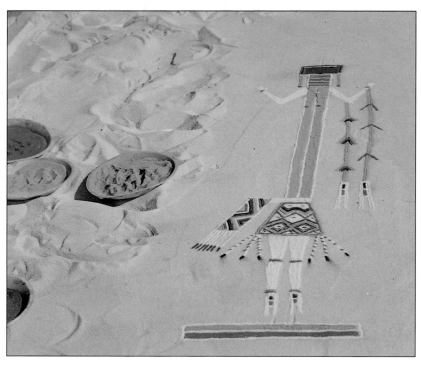

SAND PAINTINGS ARE MADE BY THE NAVAJO DURING HEALING CEREMONIES.

using rocks, gems, and minerals to make beautiful jewelry based on traditional tribal designs.

Like the many Native American groups of North America today, peoples all over the Earth continue to use the rocks, gems, and minerals of the planet's crust in many ways. From seasoning our foods and decorating our bodies to making skyscrapers and spacecraft, these natural materials remain an important part of our ever-changing world.

GEORGE CATLIN PAINTED THIS PORTRAIT OF THE DISTINGUISHED WARRIOR HE WHO CRIES WOLF IN 1834.

Rocks Named After People

Sometimes rocks and minerals are named after people. Catlinite, another name for pipestone, is named after the painter **George Catlin**, who lived from 1796 to 1872. George Catlin is well known for his paintings of early Native American peoples and their lifestyles.

SILVER AND TURQUOISE BRACELETS MADE BY NATIVE AMERICAN ARTISANS.

BIBLIOGRAPHY

Children

Eldredge, Niles, Douglas and Gregory. *The Fossil Factory*.
    Reading, Mass.: Addison-Wesley Publishing Company, Inc., 1989.

Horenstein, Sidney. *Rocks Tell Stories*. Brookfield, Conn.: The Millbrook Press, 1993.

Williamson, Tom. *Understanding the Earth*. Morristown, N.J.:
    Silver Burdett Company, 1984.

Adult

Kunz, George Frederick. *The Curious Lore of Precious Stones*.
    New York: Facts on File, Inc., 1988.

Matthews, William H. III. *A Guide to the National Parks, Their Landscape
    and Geology*. Garden City, N.Y.: Doubleday/Natural History Press, 1973.

Pearl, Richard M. Peterson *Field Guide: Rocks and Minerals*, 4th edition.
    Boston: Houghton Mifflin Company, 1983.

Sloane, Howard N. and Russell H. Gurnee. *Visiting American Caves*.
    New York: Crown Publishers, Inc., 1966.

Tilden, Freeman. *The National Parks*. New York: Alfred A. Knopf, 1986.

PHOTO CREDITS

Exploring Science: Human
Biology
Photo/illustration credits

Photography credits:

Peter Arnold: © Nelson
Max/LLNL: 17t;

© Ronald H. Cohn/The Gorilla
Foundation: 29;

© Bruce Coleman: 16t; © K. &
K. Ammann: 27b; © Frank
Brown: 36; © E.R. Degginger:
9, 12t, 14t, 35b, 41t, 44, 45t,
45bl, 48r, 55t; © John Fennell:
55; © Jeff Foott 26; © Bob
Gossington: 43r, 45m, 55b; ©
Linda Koebner: 28b; ©
Douglas Mazonowicz: 53; ©
Shaw McCutcheon: 61b©
Patricio Robles: 11t; © L. West:
27t;

Dembinsky Photo Associates:
© Skip Moody: 15l;

FPG International: 10t; © Gary
Randall 28t; © Ken Ross: 17b;
©Telegraph
Color Library: 21bl, 61t;

© Ken Lax: 9, 13, 18, 19, 20,
25, 33, 43, 59 (all photo
sequences involving
children);

© Los Angeles Museum: 56b;

The Waterhouse: © Stephen
Frink: 15r;

Tom Stack & Associates: ©
John Cancalosi: 32t, 32b, 33tl,
33bl, 35t, 35m;

Tony Stone Images: © Steve
McCutcheon: 39t; © Chris
Schwartz: 8;

©Phil Schermeister: 37;

© Visuals Unlimited: 10b, 40l,
49t, 49b; Frank Awbrey: 42r; ©
Cabisco: 39b;
© R. Feldman: 12b; © R.
Kessel: 21lr; © National
Museum of Kenya: 42l, 46l,
46r; © David Phillips: 20l, 23l;

Illustration credits:
© Laura Pardi Duprey: 16, 19l,
21, 22, 23, 24l, 25l, 29, 40, 56,
68;
© George Gilliland: 14-15b,
17r, 30, 46, 54, 58;
© American Museum of
Natural History/New York: 37t;
Illustrations by Siena
Artworks/London, England, ©
Michael Friedman Publishing
Group 1995: 11r, 24r, 29b, 31,
34, 38, 40r, 47, 48, 52, 56, 57;

Key: t=top, b=bottom, l=left,
r=right, m=middle;